Katrina Rodabaugh

Words need love too

||||| ||| ||||| ||| ||||| ||| |||||
D1520683

Coming, Coming Home - Conversations II
Western Education & The Caribbean Intellectual
George Lamming

Regreso, regreso al hogar - Conversaciones II
La educación occidental y el intelectual Caribeño
George Lamming

The Republic of St. Martin
Joseph H. Lake, Sr.

Introduction to Government
Island territory of St. Maarten
Louis Duzanson

Colorful Religion
Mini-stories of the Caribbean Church
(1701-1998)
Gerard van Veen

Big Up St. Martin: Essay & Poem
Colony, Territory or Partner?
The Cubs Are in the Field
Lasana M. Sekou

Songs & Images of St. Martin
Charles Borromeo Hodge

Brotherhood of the Spurs
(short stories, fiction)
Lasana M. Sekou

Tales from The Great Salt Pond
Esther Gumbs

National Symbols of St. Martin - A Primer
Edited by Lasana M. Sekou

Pass It On!
A Treasury of Virgin Islands Tales
Jennie N. Wheatley

Kamau Brathwaite

Words need love too

House of Nehesi Publishers   St Martin, Caribbean

HOUSE OF NEHESI PUBLISHERS
P.O. Box 460
Philipsburg, St. Martin
Caribbean

WWW.HOUSEOFNEHESIPUBLISH.COM

ISBN: 0-913441-47-3
Library of Congress Cat. Number: 00-132458

Cover design and art by Angelo Rombley
Photography: Kamau Brathwaite, CP Collection 2000; GIS (author reading at the
first National Heroes Day celebration, April 1998, Barbados).

Acknowledgement & Thanks
to the spirits of this pasture - birds, man/woman
walking; in their Thyme Bottom homes;
two-tail bulls, cows, blackbelly sheep, insects
& angels - sky, rain, dewdrops, dawn, deep sunsets
of the harmattan, the dunks; the sea
always there - marine shimmering, green
dreaming, blue-white, grey-white & sometimes
shivering, sharks skin & whales
for the help & hospitality of all these muses,
powers, the insights & inspiration
that make this collection possible;
planted & prepared, the harvest of three
DreamChad years of love & interstanding
we have here at CowPastor

Contents

Introduction

[T]he word (is) the atomic core of language. . . .
The word (nommo, name) is held to contain secret power.
- Kamau Brathwaite, *(Roots, 1993)*

In the beginning was the word; and the word was made flesh. But before the word, before sound, there was silence. The silence of dreams; the silence of memory, or "that awesome moment of wonder in which communion is made with the spiritual,"[1] as Michael Dash would put it. The silence of Xângo before he rolls out his tongue of thunder to announce the rain. The cold silence of the anvil before Ogun pounds his hammer on it to mould iron into sword. No other Caribbean poet, living or dead, understands that silence, makes us participants in, and co-celebrants of the liturgy of the word, than Kamau Brathwaite. "What the poet seems to be doing is linking a fundamentally religious notion with the process of artistic creativity," writes Dash, in his critical appraisal of Brathwaite's works.

Indeed, Brathwaite in this his latest collection of poems, *Words need love too*, invites us, not just to witness that process of artistic creativity, but to be co-creators of a new cosmos, a new genesis on these "rolling stones of the sea that gather no moss." To enter this new world, to claim this new garden, we must return to the time and space before the word. In other words, we must recapture the silence that precedes and announces the word and is later made into the word itself. Here we are in the womb of memory where dreams are born; the darkest moment before dawn, before light is born. Herein lies the "secret power" of the word, "the atomic core of language." Brathwaite, the poet, becomes a nuclear word-physicist, splitting the atom-words into neutrons, into neutrons of dreams, and from the fission he fashions a fusion that makes the inner power of the word-idea erupt like a volcano. He becomes a geneticist, working with the DNA of the word, re-discovering the word-genomes that give the dream its texture, its very life, and re-assembling them into the book of a new reality, for without dreams, there can be no reality.

"Brathwaite seems to consider reality in general in terms of a world fallen from grace; the poet's special role revolves around his awareness of this fall and his capacity to recapture the lost state through his vision," Dash continues in his analysis. That world, however, did not "fall from grace"; it was forced from grace and fell into dis-grace. Brathwaite fully understands this. That is why the role of the poet becomes for him one of reconstruction, of re-creating through the "secret power" of the word, through creative memory ("awareness" of the forcing from grace), new dreams, a new "vision" of reality, a new state of grace. Brathwaite seeks to achieve this by reconnecting with the power Xângo unleashes in his thunder, with the genius of the houngan, Toussaint L'Ouverture, with the vision of Dessalines, and the spontaneous inventiveness of jazz. This is evident in the poem, "Défilée":

> *Bright thrones have been cast down before*
> *the leaders stripped & torn from power. fled or dead*
> *Dessalines my liberator my xecutioner mon Empereur*

Dessalines did not fall from grace, but was "cast down" from his bright throne, "stripped & torn from power." The assassinated Haitian Head of State is mourned in the poem by the meatseller, Défilée, reputedly once his lover, as a "savage warrior," a visionary and powerful general, flung down from his high horse. "How they dis. member dis. honor dis. remember you," she laments and adds: "and so i pick you back each pick & pluck/a root a memory a flower." Défilée, the "madwoman," is the poet himself whose memory of Emperor Dessalines is rooted in the blood and sperm of the assassinated general and flowers into a new consciousness of history, of self.

Brathwaite was born many rains ago in Barbados. Graduating from Cambridge while in his early 20s, he belongs to that generation of Caribbean writers who found their voice in exile, like fellow Barbadian, George Lamming, with whom he shares a kindred artistic spirit. The sun had already begun to set on the British Empire in the post-war era of the early 1950s. It was a period of great political flux, and intellectual and artistic ferment, especially for scholars and other emigrants from the colonies. Frustration, alienation, and a sense of dispossession reigned amongst them, forcing them to turn their eyes homeward in an attempt to resolve, not only the issue of their identity, but more significantly of their destiny.

"Homeward," however, for Brathwaite, who dubbed himself "a roofless man of the world" shortly became a journey back to his ancestral roots in Africa. He lived and worked in Ghana from 1955 to 1962, eight years during which he sought to re-immerse himself in the culture from which he had been estranged for over 400 years. It was during this period that Brathwaite became re-baptised, shedding his Christian name, Edward, for the African name of Kamau. Recounting this "baptism of spit" in a lecture in St. Martin at the beginning of the year 2000, the poet explained that he did not drop his last name too out of respect to his mother. But the ceremony and the meaning of his new name remain fresh in his memory and form the essence of his re-integration into the ancestral world. From the "rooflessness" of his sojourn in Britain, Brathwaite found a rootedness in Africa that would sharpen his sense of "wholeness" and shape his awareness of what Dash calls the "communion with the mysterious and numinous which is absent in the historically disadvantaged New World."

It was, however, not the return of the prodigal son; nor a Garveyite "back to Africa" transposition. For Brathwaite, it was a re-connection, a re-education, even a re-baptism in ancestral waters. After eight years of immersion in those waters, he re-emerged a new person with a first-hand knowledge of his African ancestry and returned home, to the Caribbean. His memory of his roots now rekindled in a renewed self-knowledge, he could give us *Masks* (1968), not as a romantic, idealized vision of Africa, but as an existential testament to the continuity that had been truncated by slavery and colonialism. Incomprehensibly (or is it deliberately?) Dash seems to ignore this and continues to call him Edward Kamau Brathwaite, instead of Kamau Brathwaite. The meaning and power of the name in Africa is completely lost to Dash. This weighs negatively on his understanding of the works and significance of Brathwaite as a Caribbean poet.

Back from Africa, Brathwaite the historian, Brathwaite the poet, Brathwaite the literary and cultural critic, had now found new paradigms, which were actually old, in the tradition of his forefathers who saw the word as an act of creation in itself. The dislocated psyche is now "rock-steady"; it now has a history, it has become a wholesome psyche allowing the poet to conjure up his-story as a "Word-Making Man" (the title of his poem dedicated to Nicolás Guillén of *Man-making Words*): "Now we rock-steady safely in the orisha of our dreams/& yr name has become the sunsum of our ancestors/. . ./you have whispered it all, you have uttered it all/coriolan of blood, plankton of melt & plangent syllables." The secret power of the word erupts from the depths of the sea as Xângo's name is invoked: "& the sea between us yields its secrets/silver into pellables into sheets of sound/that bear our pain & spume & salt & coltrane/saying xângo/. . ./so that we learn w/you the pleasure/of walking w/our roots across the country/owners herein of all there is to see/owners herein of what we must believe/of what our hands encompass as we dream."

If we understand "dream" as memory thrown into random orbit in the mindscape of silence, of soundlessness, then we will understand the lines that immediately follow as a "naming" ceremony, as the transformative power of the word, for to name something is to claim it, to infuse it with proprietorship, with spirit: "so that together we say wind/& understand its history of ghosts/together we say fire/& again there is a future in those sparks/together comrade friend/we say this our land & know at last at last it is our home/now mine forever & so yours amigo/ours/'w/the vast splendor of the sunshine & the sunflower & the/stars."[2]

This is in the best tradition of Aimé Césaire of "Cahier d'un retour au pays natal" whom Brathwaite quotes in his seminal collection of essays, *Roots*: "I will recover the secret of epic speech and towering conflagrations. I would say storm, I would say river. I would say tornado. I would say leaf. I want to pronounce tree. . ."[3]

The creative process for Brathwaite would appear to go through four stages that dissolve one into the other: silence or pre-sound, memory, dream, and sound (word/idea/language). It may be pure coincidence that he similarly divides this volume of poetry into four sections, but in "Xângo at the Summer Solstice," we observe how that creative process is portrayed:

> Xângo cyaan go no far-
> ther. all winter long he store the sounds you hear now in
> these man-
> dolins. all through the cold hard dark he labour for this light
> & now he find it on im lip. he blow the flute he string
> im lute im rise & go again looking for his Oya

Xângo, the god of thunder, whose original climes know no winter, through the re-connecting and re-creative vision of Brathwaite, works "all winter long," and in "cold hard dark" silence, he stores (in memory) "the sounds you hear now in/these man-/dolins." From **silence**, in silence, musical notes are born in Xângo's **memory** which are transposed through creative (**dream**-like) labor to "im lip," which releases them as **sounds** of music into the flute, into the lute. The process has taken us from darkness to light, to Xângo's search for his lover, Oya. But it is a Sisyphean task that Xângo is condemned to undertake over and over again ("im rise & go **again** looking for his Oya"). So is the creative process which the poet must go through over and over again. But in Brathwaite, the process becomes the product, the four stages not only dissolve into one another, but the magic of creation becomes creation itself.

His use of dialect or as he himself has christened it, "nation-language" is not--Dash is right--a "gratuitous rejection of formal poetic devices," but has indeed been "subjected to enough of a formal re-ordering and control that it rises above the commonplace to become the language of poetry."[4] Brathwaite achieves a similar effect in "The Nansetoura of CowPastor" in which Ananse, the Spider, not only warned him of her entry into "the grave (or darkness, **si-lence**)/hidden within the clump of prickly man/-peaba & red cordea trees & countless clammacherry," but tried unsuccessfully to prevent him from taking "photograph" (**memory**) that "brought us this/past midnights with yr silent humming/the musky smell of turning in yr sweaty bed (**dream**) . . . & never never never/yr sweet mouth bash & brutalize (**sound**, words)/my sister mother o my aunt my ances-tor." The Spider then tells him in nation-language:

> no calabash or flower on my grave no nine night wake
> no forty days of journey through the salt lagoon No fru- it
> to heal this lips No okra at my hips. What happen>
> >here to me is like you vomit like a rodent in Kaneshi>
>
> market. Three hundred years I staring here under this
> spider web & bush. ananse at my door of herbs. and no-
> (w) you come disturb me with yr camera destroy the ru-
> in of my spiral with yr flash. O watch me now, my chi-
>
> ld my nephew flesh of my flash great great grandbroth-er
> from this other world. You think they dispossessing
> you? You tink you tall? you think you mouttamassiman
> Rasta, reckon you rave? You say you writin poem about
>
> slave You evva hear what Nanny tell de backra bout she
> black backside? But looka yu dough nuh! Look wha be
> <come a you! A buckra halfwhite backsite bwoy, eatin>
> dah backra culture dah backra culture eatin you!

Throughout this volume, the pattern of Brathwaite's creative process resonates with the brilliance of a Wynton Marsalis trumpet. The past is not an obscure, remote landscape, but is often juxtaposed with the present in harmonious (and sometimes, even dialectic) co-existence, to be projected as synthesis into the future with the force and energy of an Ifa priest. In "The SilverSands Poem," he stresses that transformation: "the long hard body of the rocky coast now softly floating/away into space/my eyes lifted upward to where the light of the world is/ . like a fish at last of release ./tracing itself thru the hallow . climbing thru time/to millennium."

That transformation, in fact, becomes innovation, themat-
ically and structurally, in the living tradition of jazz. This attitude
however, contains a warning; like the one issued by the Spider to the
irreverent poet/photographer who had three camera lenses smash-
ed--tradition will not tolerate arrogant prying. The wisdom of the
Spider, who hangs a "No Disturbance" sign on his grave, who wants
no fetish, no totems, no mourning, after three hundred years of star-
ing from behind his web, resides in his self-assured pride of Nanny,
in contrast to whom the artist-scholar-historian appears rather fool-
ish, without what Brathwaite himself has called "groundation."

Mercilessly, Ananse contrasts Nanny's attitude to the back-
ra, and her "black backside" to that of the artist who has become "A
huckra halfwhite backsite bwoy, eatin>/dah backra culture (while)
dah backra culture eatin you!" Bob Marley picks up on that tradi-
tion when he sang in " Time will tell": "you think you in heaven but
you're living in hell."

In "The Zoo," Brathwaite takes us into the world of the
Nigerian writer D.O. Fagunwa of *Igbo Olodumare* (translated by
Wole Soyinka as *The Land of the 1000 Demons*) where the animals
acquire human dimensions, where the ostrich is "that withered
scholar," the dodo "like someone we know. so-/phisticated uncle,"
and "clergy-penguins" are "awkward little gentlemen/. . ./posing in
black/and white. standing stock-/still." They "are merely gathered
here/so we can gape and celebrate their public idiosyn-/crasies. so we
can pause. point. peel oranges/buy buns to throw. clutch at each
other's sleeve/and feel we recognize some old acquaintance stick-/ing
out his tongue." Later, toward dusk, ". . . we lose the sense/of cage
and circumscripted freedom . . ." until "the ugly gadgets of the zoo"
are unlocked for the animals to find their freedom "in these silent
fleets now sailing heaven" released "from this harsh xile's solitude."

Brathwaite's zoo of "circumscripted" freedom is however
different from Fagunwa's forest of free-roaming allegorical beasts. It
is a "harsh xile of solitude" but at the end of the poem, a transfor-

mation, (or rather transposition), occurs: it is the human visitors to the zoo that inexorably find themselves confined, caged like the "stoic old man nodding goat" or the "polar-bears like solid smiling ghosts" or like the seals that "cannot conceal the fact that where they play or flap/is merely minor freedom for/them," while the birds and the beasts become free to sail the heavens like the mountains at the coastline "floating away into space" in "The SilverSands Poem."

Brathwaite approaches poetry, like the great African-American collagist Romare Bearden did in most of his seminal paintings; with humility, respect and a burning desire to seek light from the darkness of the truncated and dismembered roots. The technique of jazz--improvisation, poly-rhythms, free associations, etc., which Bearden, the master collagist exhibited with such lyric fluency in his works, is paralleled by Brathwaite, the genial wordsmith, especially in the last poem of this collection, "Agoue - a sequence for voice, choral chorus, music & vodounistas."

"The new graphic presentation of his poems could be seen not as eccentric doodles but as an attempt to integrate the acoustic into the written text," writes Dash in his essay on Brathwaite. Said presentation, however, is no longer new in Brathwaite; it has become his signature. No poem better exemplifies this than the title poem itself, "Words need love too." In it, the vowels are highlighted, with the "i" being represented hieroglyphically as the human eye. Silence, memory, dreams, and sound constitute the quadrangular coordinates within which Brathwaite shapes his poetic world, his creative cosmos, his word. Brathwaite knows indeed that "Words, need love too" because above anything else, he loves words, like a parent loves his children, like God loves his creatures. He cares for them, plays with them, talks to them, nourishes them, cuddles them, moulds them in his image, in the image of goodness. Even when they cannot utter a sound, he speaks to them in "baby-talk," in onomatopoeia, in sound symbols, in "video" words.

For Brathwaite, words are not just mere sounds, or imagery, or symbols; they are all that and more. They are not just incantations, evocations, invocations; they are all of that and more. They are not arranged as mere syntactic ornaments, nor as musical notes to caress our ears with the sweetness of their melody. He breaks them up, un-writes them, decants them of all earthly impurities, sifts them as if they were gold dust, re-arranges them, polishes them to bring out their original glitter, their essential luster. Then he breathes life into them and sets them free with their own intelligence, their own life, a new life, so that we can hear them, feel them, touch them, see them roam the world of his poems, naked like on creation day. In Brathwaite, words are made flesh. He re-creates them; makes them walk, makes them talk like us.

> but steep defile beyond all these. words need
> our eyes to follow them. out of their secret
> places of respect. down to the deep drown
> pools of human history that underneath yr eyes

> they need our hands to undercover them
> nourish rebel revel & at last reveal them
> our palms on their wet cheeks of future

> hold them so soon so vulnerable so soft
> and their burn
> & born

> . . .

> bringing yr lips at last out

> not to resist not to resist but kiss
> kiss shapes back into their proper pout
> & speech into their proper sounds

> & even beyond these proper sounds
> soft song soft songs
> chant canticle poem & halleluja halleluja halleluja

They sing dirges for all the unburied souls of the Middle Passage. They do the limbo as a ritual re-enactment of their tortured history and lose their shackles to dance the syncopated and syncretic complexity of the vodoun, the ponum, the tumba, the gwoka, the bachatta; to dance to Marley's reggae beat--jumping, skanking, seductively wriggling in a movement of freedom: "*o jah selassie i . o rastafari* rooted in the fields./brown brunt & burn towards the rotting/concrete city needing love/*o rotting city needing love the wheels the monstrous messengers/the raped the dead the leprous scavengers . . .*"

Words need love too represents perhaps Brathwaite's most concentrated effort at fashioning a new literary tradition out of the fragmented pieces that form the New World. He expresses this magnificently in the very opening poem of this collection, "Jerry Ward & The fragmented spaceship dreamstorie." Moving effortlessly in space and time, from Tougaloo, Mississippi of 1650 to the summer of 1983, to Tougaloo College in 1992, the slave-ships that brought our ancestors to this new continent had become spaceships that seemed to have crashed into the New World/plantation:

> *& xploded on impact/the **stars** of the ship*
> *from their commune origen scattering over a wide*
> *wide area & each part/you see/in the godness*
> *or badnage of time springing its own roots*
> *& getting on w/ its own business but preserving*
> *the memory since each was a part/ now trying*
> *to be whole/ of the original the source/with the*
> *possibility indeed the ideal intention of one day*
> *reconstructing/reconstituting the orig*
> *-inal ancestral at least symbolically at least*
>
> *metaphorically at least spiritually at least philoso*
> *-phically. so that as in space travel*
> *there cd be an evanescent but v/ real four dimensional*
> *image of the origins made out of atoms of light*
> *- a holograph? - giving (allowing)*
>
> *each one of us in our different parts a common memory*
> *& language & angel*
> *really, w/ which to speak to each other & to the world*

All two dozen poems in this volume are therefore "dreamstories," seeking to be picked up by "someone un-known & unexpected" as "one of the green shoots of metal or mental/ fragment" to be planted so that it can grow and spread and flourish "perhaps in his own work & person/ality." Brathwaite retrieves in them old themes, inserts new ones and imbues them with a regenerative vision that is as powerful as it is exciting. With extraordinary nimbleness of spirit, he crisscrosses continents and history as if he were the star of a sci-fi feature film.

As perceptive as Dash is in several aspects of his analysis of Brathwaite's poetry, his conclusions are surprisingly and fundamentally flawed in quite a few areas. There is nothing to lead us to assert that Brathwaite showed in his works in the 1980s "the frustration of the demiurgic voice in its project to create a Caribbean negritude." Similarly, there is absolutely no evidence to substantiate the claim that "Brathwaite's personal misfortune lead to almost hysterical shrieks of isolation and gloom." In fact, Brathwaite does not isolate himself, nor does he offer any poetic vistas of gloom. To the contrary, Brathwaite, himself a leading literary critic, integrates himself, his experience and his work within a truly Pan-Caribbean (one is tempted to say even Pan-African) context.

In addition, to place him at the epicenter of a "phase that is coming to an end"[5] is incongruous with the weight of the "rooted" and re-generative continuum to which he and his works belongs, and of his continuing influence on contemporary Caribbean writing. The evidence of this continuum and Brathwaite's influence are very obvious, for example, in the young St. Martin poet, Lasana M. Sekou's work, especially in "Nativity," a long, epic performance poem, in which he writes:

> *Kamau-an-found beats in warriorsilence*
> *mek night march through cosmic cadenza*
> *.(who feels it knows it. keeps ac-*
> *counting. We Keeper of counts. . . .*[6]

Brathwaite is undoubtedly aware of his own impac Caribbean letters; and he knows that his place is at the cutting edge of its aesthetics. He gives those that blazed the trail before him and with him their due, humbly acknowledging their illuminating influence on him that allowed him to "climb high into caves." This is Brathwaite's self-assessment of his own position within the literary landscape of the Caribbean. It is done without any false humility. In "Praise Song 2000" Brathwaite writes: "the moon-lipsed bays have been haunted by Walcott/the grapes & almond leaves. the goat-foot ipomea/by Frank Collymore; the sandylanes by the Hon. H A Vaughan. & in their light i climb high into caves. the stalag-/mitred brevitor. the north-point mysteries. chimera/of pale-blue & purple sea anemones."

The sea anemones were called "animal flowers" in his younger days. He, however, acknowledges that he is "too weak to stoop to catch them scoop/them up before the rebel lion wave roars/mighty in the cave holloring for koromanti. calabar/for the hollow dungeons of gorée/for the lost tribes of atlantis." Brathwaite ends this poem with glowing tribute to the star-studded cast of personalities who have become icons of Caribbean culture: "praise be to those who have recovered us our names/nourbese & allsopp of our tongues. thank you jah/for the buttapan steel pan & sparrow & bob o rastafari/chilldren & the atumpan. those who have loved us lost/lost sheep when all the merchants who wd slaughter/slaughter sleep. thank you guillén césaire wilfredo/limbo. chad. sir garfield sobers. caribbean stars."

We must invariably add: thank you too, kamau.

- Fabian Adekunle Badejo
St. Martin, 2000

Notes

[1] J. Michael Dash, "Edward Kamau Brathwaite," *West Indian Literature*, ed. Bruce King, 2nd ed. (London: Macmillan, 1995).

[2] Kamau Brathwaite, "Word-Making Man," *Middle Passages* (Newcastle upon Tyne: Bloodaxe Books, 1992).

[3] Aimé Césaire, "Cahier d'un retour au pays natal," *Roots*, by Kamau Brathwaite (Michigan: The University of Michigan Press, 1993).

[4] Dash.

[5] Dash.

[6] Lasana M. Sekou, "Nativity," *Nativity and Monologues for Today* (St. Maarten: House of Nehesi Publishers, 1988).

"Self Portrait." Digital illustration by Angelo Rombley © 1998.

JerryWard & the fragmented
spaceship dreamstorie JerryWard

remind me on Fri 14 Feb/telephone conversation
at NYU/of a talk i grieve at his College/Tougaloo, Mississippi
in 1650 about the slave trade/ middle passage

'You may recall having met me
when you lectured at a Southern Black Cultural
Alliance meeting here in summer 1983. . .'/Tougaloo
College Feb 5, 1992 i/i'm afraid/ had not writ anything
down nor was it recorded but he remembers a passage
in which (he tried to spell it back out for me on a telephone)
i said that it was as if the spaceship bringing us here
had like **crash** into the New World/plantation

& xploded on impact/ the **stars** of the ship
from their commune origen scattering over a wide wide
area & each part/ you see/ in the godness
or badnage of time springing its own roots
& getting on w/ its own business but preserving
the memory since each was a part/ now trying
to be whole/ of the original the source/with the
possibility indeed the ideal intention of one day
reconstructing/reconstituting the orig
-inal ancestral at least symbolically at least

metaphorically at least spiritually at least philoso
-phically. so that as in space travel
there cd be an evanescent but v/ real four dimensional
image of the origins made out of atoms of light
- a holograph? - giving (allowing)

each one of us in our different parts a common memory
& language & angel
really, w/ which to speak to each other & to the world
He did not 'say' in effect all this to me - he might have
said more he might have said less/ i remember

3

him saying that he often wonder what had **happen**
to my piece & what had happen to the pieces
of my piece/where/ if/when/how/ they had grown
& i thanked him/thank him for this gift
of memory so early in the morning of snow
& that it was good & wonderful (w/ clear sunlight despite the
snow) that the idea - the words - the images
had remain/had i suspect been staining in his mind
so that now he had met me so many years after/ even
tho i had forgotten

that night i think it was or must or might have been
in Tougaloo & what i had said thought & felt
that evening & had allowed it to be cost
by the wayside/ someone unknown & unexpected
had picked one of the green shoots of metal or mental
fragment up & planted
it & it had grown & spread & **flourish**
perhaps in his own work & person/ality *(recall VP casting*
my bread on other people waters?) so that as i sit
here by the roadside in this strange city so far

from flowers & the flames of canefields
& Mudda Africa walk
-in w/ me over the wooden fence & thru the ploughed
brown near Indian Ground & touching the great black
anthracite stones come out of those canefields
discovering tolmec & totomec Barabadoes
wrapp in cardboard & old half-forgotten letters
& something look like flourbags from the latex
unpredicted snowfall ('not one a my seed [the Bob Marley-song
about *'shall beg yr bread in the sidewalk'/So Jah Seh*])

and he stopp right there in the middle of the lecture
of the street because he recognize me after all these years

4

"The Watchers." Digital illustration by Angelo Rombley © 2000.

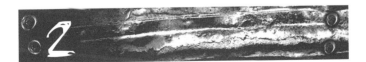

Alice in Wonderland

for Erika Ritter

White Rabbit in my work-a-day black sleep
you look to time to lure me out

to peep and ponder at the wonder-
land that lighted up the garden of your heart

How I had long to know how time
and lonely arts had lighted up the garden of your heart

And so I fell. when following up the thought

But while my heart was upside-down in air
(not-knowing child. not time-

suspecting them) I see you disappear
through key-lock garden doors

and find my heart still pounding after yours
shut out by unexpected locks of hum-

drum time

How I had long to scout beyond the work-
a-day to find the lighted wonder of your heart

But changeling sleep and wonder-
land White Rabbits will not
last. and when I wake
I find no time to follow up the key-
hole cue that speak between our hearts.

But you had thrown away the golden key and left time
heart. less in the now no-wonder dark-

ness of your heart

7

Poem for Esse

for Dofoë

Shape subtly through the wandering
months. the moon appears tonight
one more refashion & again renewed

an agony of clearest burning brightly bourne
Mother. mild as this moon
bend thy lips now to this child. thy daughter

that she here may receive
the compassionate murmur of water
its invincible serenity of silver. the disposition

of the lamb
And in the land of traitors & lechers
where men's words may be prompted by passion

or pride or the promise
of riches. in the land of the trumpeting lion
let her never be dumbfounded

Papak

The dream gripping his throat
with a groan startles the old

lecher out of his sleep
to a waste of white linen

the bed covered with moon
-light. He is out in a boat

with a fat girl with black cold
thighs and his heart is hooked in her hot meat

She is the first of his women
Soon he is bloat

-ed with them. His attacks become bold
er and bolder He cut the throats

of their love though there was no
one he wanted to keep

Now he is old and he can't sleep

Vulture

She's black but prefers to be brown
it's as simple as that

just like you

turning old would prefer to be young
her eyes are dark but he dreams them blue

lovers love golden curls he believes
rather like you

and why is my voice so husky she grieves
I would rather trill like a bird. true-

pitch. slanting the heavens. than mourning
in leaves the passing and pain of this soft passive

love. What new
worlds to conquer. Columbus not down-

hearted Caliban is who she is after
rather like you

Boy at the Blind School

'Professor by the window, if you
Will pause a moment from your
Murmuring. . . .'

The boy addressed looked
up. I say 'looked up'. altho
it wasn't that at all. He listened
up. if words wd have it so

His eyes were like dark empty
pools waiting for rain. His head was serious
and smooth. but blunt and strangely helpless
in the rain . the boy was sight. less. blind

He listened to me. waiting
the large book he was holding
open. printless. in his hand

His smooth head travelled slowly
side to side. ever so slightly
like a snail's. His fingers
interrupted. softly nervous. paused

                                    I'd come in just
                              to say goodbye. But now
                        what could I say? Here in his hands
                         he treasured texts I could not read
                          here was this face that could not see
                        Goodbye. What did departure mean
                     to him who all life long lived with arrivals
                      & goodbyes? Each object of his touch
                    meant everything when touched and was caressed
                          for secrets. and discarded only in x
                       -treme distress. to deal with new arrivals

11

His mind
was like the dark sky of stars
and like a good abstrac
-tionist. he knew their places
knew them everyone. And if one little
point drop out. he'd miss
it instantly. and in the in
-stant reconstruct the scheme - yes
- had to - until each beam & painful throb press
on him as before

So is my going from him on this morning. '*How
will you. . .*' His hand
touch mine. The blank
face listen. I could not tell if he knew me

But like a ship proceeding down the dark-
ness in a fog. no cheeks. no faces. no familiar land-
marks. I say goodbye to him
and drifted down the dumb & silent river
the little left between us. nothing new

Blanche

each guest of the year
> has stripped skin off from around her eyes
> until there are no secrets

> she washed her linen in the yard . towels
> that have known holier days. sheets
> ripped & sperm. pyjamas
> bloodied from the bladder of her brother

> but in the wind. these appear private & unreal
> flying for all the world
> to see. flying in the face of words
> to hear. outpacing their shadows like ghosts

so that each guest
> harbourmaster auctioneer city-
> sick solicitor. the honey-
> mooning couple peach & pear. flunked theo-
> logical student. no-paying hippie

believes
> that she has climb them to a well-
> scrubbed room. its bedstead steady to its task
> the door-locks safe w/their secrets

Dread

for Margaret Gill & remembering H A Vaughan

The law and its punitive munuments
   has been like a heavy hammering all these

      years. nails into mortal . the mortal
      into the unrelenting echo of the coffin

I have worn this mist and dead
   head heat of some blond barber's chair

      from fleet street . some voyeur
      from around the inns of court

      and have become all voice and forehead
      bland and fear . even the windowframes

      and frowns prevent my seeing fields
      gardeners the city's noisy carousels

      the dead bird fountain near where lovers lie
      at night . the soda fountain further down
      the light where they first meet

I am allowed in these old wooden mansions of the lex
      a woven fan of grass . this shuddering electric
      monster imitating wind in trees . but no real

      breeze. no sky's blue story cool of birds
      no caveat where i can really dream

This man before me now
      from dungeon wrack and police lock-up
      clammacherry cell . his clothes all stale
      his eyelids sale from too march sleep

      too little food and fond-
      ness in the jail . the black skin chalk
      for lack of rain. the sergeant charging

rape me lud . persistent poverty

I squint towards him

woman?

flesh?

a subtle shaft perfume?

a swimming fish in lighted glass he fail?
his dead hoot running in the long live grass?
a child perhaps? a son he love? someone to fetch

him smile?
a scrap of bread he build sometime before the flood?
a window selling books . calling for trust

for trade for trees x
-change of eyes?

there is no echo back
he looks bars thru me . metal
fears . he sees the clock . no sun
the calendar is wasted years

the harbour rock. rock.stone. blood.less guitar
the mockingbird singing that he isn't fraid karl

the studdering electric razor
in my shaven glass . for what it is

a ban upon the mild november's seas
its memories of summer booze and laid-up breeze
the stay of xecution in the distant unforgiving trees

so that he hardly hears my dead wig voice
pause at the bar and falter
son?

it almost reaches . says

ten years

Bread

Slowly the white dream wrestles to life
hands shapen the salt and the foreign cornfields
the cold flesh kneaded by fingers
is ready for the charcoal for the black wife

of heat the years of green sleeping in the volcano
The dream becomes tougher. settling into its shape
like a bullfrog. suns rise and electrons
touch it. walls melt into brown. moving to crisp

and crackle. breathing edge of the knife of the oven
noise of the shop. noise of the farmer. market
on this slab of lord. on this table w/ its oil-skin cloth
on this altar of the bone. this scarifice

of isaac. warm dead. warm merchandise. more than
worn merchandise
life
itself. the dream of the soil

itself

flesh of the god you break. peace to your lips. strife
of the multitudes who howl all day for ijs saviour
who need its crumbs as fish
flickering through their green element

need a wide glassy wisdom to keep their drowns alive

and this loaf here. life
now halted. more and more water add-
itive. the dream less clear. the soil more distant
its prayer of table. bless of lips. more hard to reach

w/ penn-
ies. the knife

that should have cut it.   the hands that should have
broken open its victory of crusts
at your throat.   balaam watching w/ red leak-
ing eyes. the rats
finding only this young empty husk
sharp-

ening their ratchets. your wife
going out on the streets. searching searching .
her feet tapping. the lights of the motor-
cars watching watching round-

ing the shape of her girdle.   her back naked
rolled into night into night w/out morning
rolled into dead into dead w/out vision
rolled into life into life w/out dream

Défilée

for Joan Dayan & Djene Small

About noon on Friday October 17, 1806, not three years after he was declared Head of State &
Emperor, Jean Jacques Dessalines, the Liberator of Haiti, successor of Toussaint Louverture, was
assassinated by soldiers from the South on the road from Marchand two miles to Port-au-Prince,
the capital. His shot & stabbed body was stoned & torn to pieces by his murderers & left, it is
said, to be found & taken for burial by the "madwoman" Défilée (Défillée), a meat seller
(vivandière) reputedly once the Emperor's lover

Bright thrones have been cast down before
the leaders stripped & torn from power.   fled or dead
Dessalines my liberator my xecutioner mon **Empereur**

my lover of Pont-Rouge like this
who break the bread w/bloody hands who tear
the nation flag from Blancechette & make it red

& make it blue. unfurl it new. where now it stands
for slave & bloody cloth & resurrected
bone. who throw the whiteman down

from his plantation towerhome at Cormiers at Vivières
the crackle axe of musketeers
against La Crête

Now here w/out yr head w/out yr virile hands. bereft
of Claire Hereuse. of balls. bereft of eyes. yr ears cut
off from music. matross. cannon. chasseurs

racheteers

tendernesse of love pulled down into this mud
where no clouds move
across the sky where no stars stare

where no wind blues where no sun shines
upon yr skin. where the red blood un
-gurgled from yr throat now flows & flowers flowers

O Dessalines so so cut up

18

                                    O splendid coat so splendidly cut down

Cows on this dry pasture all my strife provide me meat goats.
blackbelly sheep are here. hens. turkeycocks jack rabbits rare but
sweet. swift bones so full of life

each morning to yr door i bring this little covered heap of victuals.
the long dark face i so adore. the fingers on the plate the morsel to
your lips my love my pain

plain sacrifice of my sweet flesh upon yr palate
yr plasaj. O savage warrior how you chop me up
you chop me down into the howling hot prostrations

of yr love
O how I love each shaken silken golden moment
of yr power

     Now into this coarse pig-stain macoute I carry w/me everywhere
               for years it watch my rape. witness

          my parents death. how Rochambeau come kill
            down all my breddas and my two only suns
            inside the Cahos mountains. trick Toussaint off

          to France till i go mad w/all this blood
            this trekking death down in this mud
                      betrayals

               maroon dark nights
               mornings of rendezvous
quick anxious crossing of the river coming back to you

     mules on the edges of high trails of mountain passes
my mind cooing w/the mourn of woodoves all day long
          watching myself like blackbirds on the floor

     criss-crossing imperfections in myself made mad
       w/manananse working working working cross
          the starbed strawbed ceiling of my floor

Now sit i down beside you in yr pool of blood
w/seven wailer demons in my head poor fool
to let them fling you down like this from yr high

horse. yr vision of a people marching on out of this
dungeon hearse of slavery into some proper light
no blight no more upon this twisted crop of niggers

on the land

po fool they cut you down before the morning crow
before the crowd that might have save you
gather on the road from Marèchand two miles

to Port-au-Prince

the meat they make of you I cannot sell
tho i sell sutler meat at Ogoum all my life
the fragments of yr body's dream I can but touch

O cruel piece by piece I can but gather from the entrail
entrance of the knife. there is no peace here
gaps & gashes like hot milk boil. ing over
& the furnace burning our tomorrows spoil our race

Duclos my love I cannot find yr face
this is your head wuhloss my love my love
how tenderly i love these harsh Dahomey
scars. the whipmarks on yr back. the prison bars

you break with these once hands from which you flame
is this one eye i find wrapped in the grass of years?
i cannot find the tongue you kiss me with & spit me wit
and when you spurn me. turn me out. i sit down at yr

door & wait for morning take me down to Fort St-Clair
or bring me back into the bed & spur & warm of you

this lip torn from yr skull I find near clammacherry
bushes here. its strip of skin still living so it seems

to sneer where it shd smile. mile after mile i walk
w/you mile after mile i walk for you mile after mile
i fight i hurt i heal O ride Arada ride. this is your **angel**
bone this is yr broken hand. the ruby ring

still blinking on the flinger O this can this can never be
how they dis. member dis. honour dis. remember you
assoun my bell my open door my lover

               and so i pick you back each pick & pluck
                       a root a memory a flower
            the toes back to the fit of instep & the ball
                    bearing weight of ankle

                          bone

                let the one foot if it be one
               foot walk quickly down the road
         let the slip hips dance. fit fairly into place
                  around the ready loins

      let us make love again & laugh the belly there the guts
          the navel strings the high kite of the noon
            remembering yr ancestors & fate

        assemble me yr lungs again so you may breathe
            & shout commands. turn the horse round
       & gallop off to victory to à Bois-Caiman & moon

        let me ride with you général. let me ride with you
                in these dark eyes i will restore
in this fine head i plant here in this place **of** burial

          O Dessalines O Dessalines gangan
          O magic makandal & sun & flag
              plaçage . nanchon

Words Need Love Too

epithalamium 14 february 1998 for DreamChad
w/closing stanzas set to music & sung to us by Gabby on the Atlantis Terrace,
Bathsheba, facing the long shores of Guinea

you crush my skull
you force o open cry
my mouth. red teeth. the deep thought of the gullet

o words. need love. love too

you strip the child
clothe the thin offspring of my loins
in cast-offs of indignity

so words. need love. love too

How to make sense
of all this. all this pain. this drought
scramble together vowels jewels that will help
you understand will help you understand these rain.
these rain. these rain. less

words . need love . love too

imaginings
you don't don't always clearly hear thru glass
green open fields of memory. the low blue sky

above these pleasures

mist . rainclouds . thunder . harmattan . eternal
pastures . blues . the smell at last of rain
from distant sugar factories from far africa

Words need love too

brown head of the rain-grass lies down w/the rain
easing the pain of all this all this all-night lashing rain
& the steel electric white-lake fork-eyes of the lightning

22

under the nameless guava tree
the rain-grass settles down into a perfect circle
pale pale green pool in its dispassion

Words need love too

the cocks . the black face clocks stirring to dawn
upon the wire mesh larder among the midnight teenage
cockroach children & the dirty plates

first footfall of our mother on the wooden floor
these drum-head drum-beat drumbeats like runnnning
thru our life along this corridor from sea from torn

white wave. white crabs upon the beach the paling
backyard rocks. the sun hot red brick steps
into the house. our father open door

fresh light fresh bread
the passage running to the white bright street
bicycle bells st patrick's angelus

the women selling singing w/their trays the donkey
brays the morning signing in. hibiscus dew flesh cold
but getting warm looking more red

& coral . the commandante turkey drakes
swelling swelling swelling swelling
gobbering from their first soft featherous silver grey

into these great alarums

                                    Words need love too

                        own their own valleys vowels
                                            precious
                        in-holdings choices chalices

            how the As open up the fathers doors
            make crystal thru the sky . daylight as cirrus
            cloud & arctic cold jet stream. working

all nights as jewels stares & stars
green lakes
bright flasking rivers. curled quiet rivulet

& glaciers. chipped scented ice in cones. caves
deep within the limestone soil of sea anemone
the water animalia flowers here happy & at last

Words need love too

A taking back the anger anguish at this prime
of peace

E bringing showers' blessing on this place
George Lamming's novels. Walcott's carafes
of poetry like Dominica river water. Deep wells

of Gabby songs like waterfall. his voice of clear
aubade. Amalaclava Kaieteur
Dunns River Falls. Lost Lovers Leaps

the mill at Boscobell
the long eternal sea-sound cliffs of ruin
ancestors along the East Coast road

Words need love too

the tief that smile
that eat the crispous bread & mellow pear
& drink the canejuice wine

watch the crack liquor weather change across
the fields & when the early morning loudly
rains. the over-arching blow

of god made magic from the mounds of cloud
& light & light itself. his silent singing colour

curv-

ing from the storm itself into these seven towers

o jah selassie i   . o rastafari rooted in the fields
brown brunt & burn towards the rotting
concrete city needing love

o rotting city needing love the wheels the monstrous messengers
the raped the dead the leprous scavengers the metals you deposit pollutions
minister in all this wordsworth vanishing upon this bridge

of life o broken now inglorious sounds o broken & incongorous woods
o words so shoved about so worn we cannot slip yr sandals on
& wear them in the bleeding streets of chance o claude mckay o hilton

vaughan o nuclear xplosion of all mighty sparrow nicolás guillén
my brother martin martin luther king & andrew salkey william
butler yeats. how can we tell the dancer from the dance?

& when the cane is cut. at night the stars come
silver down to where the canetops are
so low you hear their tick & singing crickets

comments

& sometimes in the silence distance
the slow misty drift of comets at their long

disasters

and O so precious are my lovers. cool

louvres

soft skin of pastures
agave. rain-grass. fern. the goat-foot ipomea

lambs

wool. black belly sheep. ships
in the harbour. reflections in the water
names dancing necklaces

shimmering like mandolins of dews. rain
drops. the rising orange sun inside them .
crabs. the breadfruit's casket skin of ancestors

the cats eye snapshot open to the light
the way my aunt at 90
smiles. the thousand thousand miles she travel

w/us to be here

here in her little yard
where she don't let she mauby get too sweet
are lilies she will light tonight. spinach

both red & green
piaba. peas. pigeon & gunga
& long duck-wallow beans

the pharoanaic waving shade of her bananas
by the paling of another world
one last green almond leaf still clinging

to its naked branch like a cicada feeding in the wind
thick mango darkness in the ackee tree. the faithful
limes outside her sleeping window

the dapple golden-apple of the gods
again the breadfruit of the ancestors
the coconut that's always taller than most other trees

pastor trees xcept
the royal palm but photos better than them all others
be. cause she is a dancer

these golden hulls of shuttered leaves. what psalms
what songs what mysteries among these blades
of western light. what jade pomegranate glitter .
all these the jewels that the Lord has made

& so to **u** my nus. my love

yr deep Maroon Trelawny names
Zion. Byall. Thistle. Sweet Bottom. Accompong

Old German Town. the Congo koumbla places
of the leopard & the lions manes
yr reverences yr hopes prayers sing-

ing jump-up. playin dominoes or draughts
or pan or moaning kites in heaven
eatin coocoo w/yelllow yelllow butter. sweet

aloes

growin on the stony hill. yr brother spear-
in lobster catch-
in fish along the last green opening to the blue

just by the entrance to St Lawrence Gap
& swimming out to sea at evening
along the long long golden everlasting highway
to the setting sun

but steep defile beyond all these. words need
our eyes to follow them.   out of their secret
places of respect. down to the deep drown
pools of human history that underneath yr eyes

                    they need our hands to undercover them
                    nourish rebel revel & at last reveal them
                    our palms on their wet cheeks of future

                    hold them so soon so vulnerable so soft
                                        after their burn
                                           & born

          that early tearing cry. that open mouth-shape morn
                             -ing w/its dark space of world
          howling from void to violence of what will become

                             yr teeth yr tongue
                    shreds torn at least to text to silence
                                              speech

the skull this egg of bone
still growing growing growing
bringing our lips at last out

not to resist not to resist but kiss
kiss shapes back into their proper pout
& speech into their proper sounds

& even beyond these proper sounds
soft song soft songs
chant canticle poem & halleluja halleluja halleluja

all this. all these. words need
clouds. bread. sunlight. yr roof above its head
love too. words need love too

"Eve the beginning… " Digital illustration by Angelo Rombley © 1999.

The Zoo

for Erika Ritter

The stoic old man nodding goat
the rear-foot knock-kneed antelopes
w/ slow translucent deep autumnal water-
colour eyes

Grave birds. vulture and raven
rook and all sorts of crows
hawks like hook councillors
and the ostrich. that withered

scholar. camel-like. on knobby
knees & xact feet. the dodo
like someone we know. so-
phisticated uncle. and the cats

these velvet devils. nervous leopards
tigers of the dream w/ large black
paws for pillows. the blue electric panther

w/ yellow moonlight eyes. smoulder-
ing aloof. and the lions sitting
in the sun w/ dozing stretched-out golden thunder

Then these queer creatures. the little boar-
rhinoceros w/ stumpy tusks and bony
face pushed permanently into flattened

fifths. the top-notch vert-
ical giraffes w/ arrogantly tip-toe heads
and parakeets w/ cries like falling plates

and then the awkward little gentlemen
the clergy-penguins. posing in black
& white. standing stock-

still. w/ blinking pale pink
eyes and help-
less flaps. even their transformation into duck-sleek

underwater innocence
like that of seals. the seals
themselves like large sad shell
fish. clinging to the rocks in lieu of shell

cannot conceal the fact that where they play or flap
is merely minor freedom for
them. that all these birds and beasts .

the polar-bears like solid smiling ghosts
squatting to their necks in yell-
ow water. crack-

ing nuts. the monkeys. active lion-rats
alert. red-bottom'd india-rubber acrobats
picking the family fleas
or swinging one-hand hellos from a pole

the flap-ear'd bumpy-headed dusty-coloured
locomotive elephants w/ small
savannas on their backs. flexing their hose-
pipe nose and grinning for a bun

are merely gathered here
so we can gape and celebrate their public idiosyn-
crasies. so we can pause. point. peel oranges

buy buns to throw. clutch at each other's sleeve
and feel we recognize some old acquaintance stick-
ing out his tongue. our next-door neighbour the orang-

outang

                But towards dusk we come upon flamingoes
             w/ delicately fashioned bent and coloured chinese
                  heads. w/ necks like poured and curved

opaque Venetian glass
w/ red-reed legs and sunset-softly-tinted coral-coloured
wings

here on this water where they feed
continually splashing silence on their slender
stilts and still protesting at the solitude

w/ their surprising tints. we lose the sense
of cage and circumscripted freedom. the geometric
zebra eating goat-wise at the wall

Here by this gentle llago. these flamingoes
Court of pleasant mandarins
these miles & miles of fragile sibilantly feeding herds

these fishers of such fine perfection
they scarcely splash
a sound

un
-lock the ugly gadgets of the zoo
release the leopard and the kangaroo

so that the eagle finds again his utmost edge
the polar bear
his berg

the monkey hanging one-hand down
forgets his act. and
falls. the flopping seals become sea-cats

again. torpedo-shape w/ whiskers
and lions stretch and roll their golden thunder down
the quivering river of the crocodiles

And we this autumn evening falling
see in our minds the pink flamingoes rising

and rising wish them well. for well

we know their wings bless bird and beast
and pray the nervous cat. the do
-cile dog. the never-changing camel

find in these silent fleets now sailing heaven
release from this harsh xile's solitude with
-holding them

Yao

Always when hungry
The lamb will bleat
The lion will roar
The dog will fawn
On his master
But to whom does the stranger
Return when touched by disaster?

The Silversands Poem

how is the sound of this south sea so soft
of the hurricane
how so in a hurry to alter the landscape . to let fish slip
under the silence
of nets . to let the sand flurry this afternoon
where we walk on the dunes
waiting for the fisherfolk of ourselves to return
to the land . to recover the harbour

the trip-feeted ipomea catches my foot in its green
upon white as i turn
from all this loud & this labour of water
the glittering blue
of this southernmost coast of our island

and as i enter the grotto
of casuarina seagrape & memory . all that sound
is lost . the sea tossing & glittering .
the wind blowing across it . the reefs of white horses .
how gentle & slow the sand now under my feet
soft as sorrow

and this grotto receives me like water . breathing
the light green of the casuarine . the sharp curled ear
of the seagrape . the cave of these ancient trees
deep underwater where i raise my hands slowly
like swimming . my hands and then my lost
feet moving into this pendulum

the long hard body of the rocky coast now softly floating
away into space .
my eyes lifted upward to where the light of the world is
. like a fish at last of release .
tracing itself thru the hallow . climbing thru time
to millennium

36

Agwe

The rolling stone of the sea gathers no moss
Fish boats and avirons are his symbols
and lambí the horn of the Xemes Indians

The lambí's whorled pink is the ear of the sea
it can hear what the god whispers
and it will pass on his messages

Once Christophe of Haiti heard of these messages
he blew on the conch's horn and a storm arose
that liberated Haiti . obliterated Haiti

Even today this lwa loves the sound of gun-
fire. the boots of marines. the stuttering tongue
of the cannon. His colour is blue

If you wish to see him. sit on a chair
and pretend to be rowing. or take a white sheep
on the first day of the year. the first clear

day of the year. and kill it among the freshwater pools
near the sea & its dark tears. Make sure
that the white wolf of surf gets hold of the carcass

And once it is floated. get well away from the beaches
No one must observe how the ghosts of the Kings
of Dahomey come striding ashore these red reaches

Requiem

for Boris Ord conducting in King's College Chapel, Cambridge

Like quick glass wave in shingle
the tuning of the strings
as I mount the rock my rostrum
My look of silence and my hands

poised on the tide of singers like a net
the rustle and uprising of the choir's grace
above the drift of strings
and bright the wave breaks song

Silence again. The sea
retreating over violins and swelling steeply
into brass and burst again of song
And look she leaps

clear of the choir's crest
the dolphin voice
the single crop of song
caught in my net of hands

Bird rising

for Nailah Folomi Imoja & Sandra the Princess of Chichén Itzá

Until it come to the time for the great myriad bird
the Mithurii

to begin its ascent . its challenge against the earth
the paradoxical oracle of wind . the wings beating
unchaining. out-

boarding. as seamen might say
the great breast ruffled & rising

as in all the great legends
and this happening here before me
under me now wonderfully surrounding me now

the white silver louvered feather shift
& chevron stretching out across the sun-

light into the pale almost like rainbow mist
of its ending. the great terrible beauty & beating
we have always heard about

beating beating beating upward & froward
the planks of its shape shivering

at first like a ship . like a dhow
then spheering down into smooth
as we scool up. wards

> Now the first hills and the darker mountains of english
> the sea below all shard & silver like our shadow
> the beacon topaz eyes un
> -blinking even through all the shudder
>
> the wings now stretched across all space
> open. ly & awesomely . so that we are not beating
> any. more but *ahh* sailing . something like sing
> -ing because at last I have been able to nuse

39

all the wounds of the language
as long as I lay them out softly & carefully. like these unfluttering feathers of song
like the sea below turning into a grey ball of twine

without fishes or sperm

like the darkness no longer lingering above us
but we moving towards it as part of its fuse
& its future . the àxé & ayisha of sails one last time
in our ears. the earth gone a long time

now from the green spur arrogance of john crow mountain
strange
not even the memory of a veiled carefree river
in these high places. too far up now for sunsets

through all this rain & distance
in our eyes. the oars of sleep through the silence
the metaphor at last afloat in the feathers
almost alight in the darkness

Descending Gardens

for Elisheba & Ngugi wa Thiong'o

From this high bough of glistance
stretch of air
spinning in splendour down daylight arriving

under the moon. the dark
broken into the ice of stars slowly losing
their lustre

the great bird circling down through the high cloud
buffeting & like ploughing once more
into a memory of water of water

we had almost forgotten
slippering sipple over the white roof of rain
seeing where it begins its sprinkle   the wind louder

now more buffeting of cloud . the fusilage
of feathers shuddering into great
plumages . coigns . valleys . canyons of what is now

blue space . the sea at last recognized . remembered like a blue
awhile
more like a wheel now . still distant

& dreaming between thunders
the whales at last almost here with their wrinkled
centuries of skin. more blue. some green

widening out of their indigo
the great old ancient legendary wings
slanting & flattening out towards this new

planet . as the eyes . all this night still unblinking . smelling
earth . nest . rock . song
crying the forthcoming distance of ages . re-

turning to what might be. come agony. stone
walls. weatherfalls. even beaches unrolling their
blankets & reefs . their white water

people walking into their various businesses . boys
leaping into the blue
crack of ocean . gallileos of gardens all looking up. up-

wards towards us from where they have carve
their speckled circles & squares . flowers
even birds. tree. top flamingoes . can you believe it

animal eyes looking evening towards our arrival
our shadow at last travelling over the brown lineage
of ploughed land . cloudless

of rain . loud in our praises . raising even rising
the voices of grasses . lambs
of withholding . with. holding . for-

giving . no

longer anger . blackbelly sheep . feeling stronger
& stronger . no
longer that stranger of space in the now spoken

language of certain. re-
newed in the vigour of this smooth unexpected re-
turning . door-

ways at last so it seems without danger
opening onto the rain. drops of DreamChad's long line of clothes-
line's long line of headlights

along the long running narrow
line of the causeway . each one a tomorrow
of rain. bow & full of the sun. of the morning

Esplanade Poem
for maria damon

o no no no. no ill. ill wind. no ill
in. tent. no dis

. respect. no dis
-content. the open outboard strings of a falaise guitar

no praying mantis dragons swimming in the water
no scenes of velvet seas no fishers
drudging to their moses boats

no tossing waves no sweet & scented ozone flowers
no pearl lost sons returning to the beaches
in little littered shells

no judge no weather cock admiring the weather
no crocodile of catholic cathedral acolytes
leading the linen prayer

no pick no pack no chain-gang following no boss
the rolling stone of the sea gathering no moss

for two white tourisses is walkin along the book
of the beach along Bay-
shore as they call it now. by the Esplanade

in front of our Government Head. quarters
one. a man. is fat on top & bare-
breasted w/hope & toil-

ing south to lemonade & feathers. the nex
a matron woman. is talking her toll in the opposite
direction. go-

ing slow. ly north towards Brown's Beach
where i grow up. where we so sweetly use to live
she wears white slacks neatly out of the reach

of her ageing. & a dark tamarind-colour t-shirt
& dark wrap-around dark glasses & a red Tiger Woods
golf cap with the hard curve ridge over the fear. less

eyes

                              Four blacks is sweepin the beach
                                  whe they walkin.   their eyes reach
                      -in no farthere than the dazzling sand that they weep

                      -in w/their coconut brooms & bristlin amber brushes
                                  and tho they have parents frenns & relatives
                                  over in away. there appears to be no bridge

                                  no no horizon for them here where
                          pleasure craft of ivory sails & IMF graffiti yachts
                          splash shifting hulls & nodding decorated masts

                                  into the placid water. & where the gaudy tails
                          of cruise ship whales lie deep inside the harbour
                                                                        water

                          It might seem that the sand-sweepers' labour
                                  always is here. on this Sahara strip
                                        of the holiday Indies

                          whe they must work every morning's worth
                      morning's worth morning's worth morning's worth
                          coming down from the BayLand in brown khaki

                              shirts & blue baggy trousers & brooms
                  to this clear azure glitter of promise & salt liquid lips of
                              their wages speaking to them from spirits

                                        they don't even hear

The tourisses don't speak to them neither
as they pass thru the morning
tho there's sometimes a nod or a quick look of guilty

44

lie-

contact. their cruise shipping eyes already bonded
& bound on a far different differing journey
So the bare-breasted man. his fat flesh beginning

to redden. thinks
of his WTO woman at home all the way out in michelin
Michigan. or by the great concrete gate

of the Minneapolis stone-
falls. where the great east. ern rivers of North
American plenitude begin. & won-

ders if she has brought in the milk & the fat
cat out of the fur-
nace. And the middle-age matron in t-shirt

behind the dark glasses gleam-
ing is dream-
ing - believe-it-or-not - of the black-

belly sheep she see on the sea
of the pasture rounn behine the police station
at Oistins only a few days before. call-

ing her chilldren home

and she wondering now what all these years mean - the
rhyme & the reason -
the waters surrounding & drown. ing her season

                    The sweepers of the beach also have their sweet hearts behind
                                                              their heads
                                    high up in the BayLand & Beckles
                                                              Hill rock

                                                  o proud race of car
                          painters. cricketers. small farmers. almshouse

attendants. gardeners at the valoriously local
elementary schools and the young pupil teacher

teaching dudes . they take careful stock
of the goats in the cowpen. the henna hens
on the cob. the sweet pea glowing like a sun-spot lens
in the bush. before they lock-up & come-down

here to the beach
out of the reach of their friends & the cattle
the tell-tale cackle of the turkey-cocks in the yard
& the children crying out in anger

it seems. for more love & more calcium
and so they never look up. they never look up at all all
the time they are here on this Bayview beach
as they call it these days. sweeping the sands of Dee

But i can tell you this . i can tell you this

all these have i seen
recorded & passing before me along the long line
of the morning

are not passing along the beach
& the water & the open sky
-line alone. the eye

might think so from this distance
in the full green view of the ships & the gentle blinks
& whispers of waves

by the Govvament Head. Quarters & the fret
-work Prime Minister's Office of flowers & flags
& an ob

-long ornamental wrought-iron pool
where as I say I 'attended'
the Bay Street Boys Primary School

                              - and perhaps who knows it ought to be so

But in their different ways. different part-
ners of ways out here on this beach
of the ages

all two. four. six. teem of them. here & not here home
& not home . criss-
crossing these ports & these tossed pages

of history

are walking their walk or sweeping the sand
of the morning . re-
reading their childhood's last howl. their lost

tropical passages
hiding their hopes where their homes
are. where the rolling stone of the sea gathers no moss

Praise Poem 2000

It's so difficult to start like all over & over again. the
egg dead in its locked cell. the heart so full of moon
it will soon burst

from my stretched bed my eyes open again & for the last
time on the marine blue. the Caribbean colours
of our royal sea. the waves breaking white outside the

window

i have tried so long to properly describe these things
the sea's ceaseless sound & colour. how its waters
snake these coral beaches & how the sunlight lights

them. they burn white fire along the sapphire shore
i am lucky to have been happy here. loved
by water. was fish in it for years & years so long

it seem it wd not end. so strong
I'm one-on-one with whatever tide. sink-
ing to the surface of the sand like a sea-

horse or star-fish & all my mothers alive
& glittering like leaves. the tin-roof hats. the sudden
steeples of the churches. a piece of yellow

fluttering glass on britton's hill

each day at dawn the fishers set out in their boats
i know the sound they make. the creak
of oars in wedlock. the water-splash. the groan

of rope through mattock. dark voices on dark water
the later higher pitcher cries of children come to bathe
& bomb the beach w/ sandballs. ndebe masks of sand-

face. just like ndebe craftsmen. the dark eyes dark. x-
cited. the red lips red. protruding. the little black face
white & enigmatic

we remember all this lost & on the way across
atlantica. apes jimmy-athletes gyimmums & moko-
jumbies. the moon-lipsed bays have been haunted

by Walcott . the grapes & almond leaves the goat-
foot ipomea by Frank Collymore. the sandylanes
by the Hon H A Vaughan. and by their light

i climb high into caves. stalag-
mitred brevitor. the north-point mysteries. chimera
of pale-blue & purple sea anemones. animal flowers

as we call them never fading from our memory for ever
even though I am too weak to stoop to catch them scoop
them up before the rebel lion wave roars

mighty in the cave hollorin for koromanti. calabar
for the hollow dungeons of gorée
for the lost tribes of atlantis for my lost mother

my long last father. for my golden
wife. my thrilldren all left saltless on the beaches
of their sound. the muses I have loved
the muses loving me amen amen amen

what pools dry wither in the noonday sand
what rocks bleed unconsecrated circumcisions
beyond the reaches of the salt lagoon

halloo for stars above the casuarina trees
halloo for River Bay. the sky in stranded pools. soft
liquids among pebbles. the midnight

dreaming frogs we watch who watch us as . as children
we arrive at hoom. they tick all night like stars
while waters wash me slowly from yr shore to this soft

point of pink where sound returns again cicada bamboo
mile-tree casuarinas the sea-grape slope against the
sand. the blowing softly whispered dune

where we make life all afternoon

it means so little now
returning here to know this still so clear so strong
so will-endure while you in contrast. even while you

thought you strongest - strangest of ironies is it not?
how those DreamStories must have known it known it
known it all along - the knife the blinded

eyes. the twisted bone the bitter bittern parts
Haul me back on. to the plaza garcía
lorca. for i don't want to see my love live now dead

wife struggling for breath. strangled by the multi-
national hands of pain of shadows flickering her heart
like you i cannot bear to see the blood of Ignacio

in the sand . And at the end of the rain
of the foreday forest of morning
the leaves catching flame. all the early

birds of the air playing flute playing piccolo
clear as the throat of a green bottle drinking blue water.
halloo for the trees. the casuarinas'

standing ghosts. halloo for the scars
of those that have recovered us our names
nourbese & allsopp. bruce st john's studyation

50

in our pebble tongues. thank you olodumare
for the buttapan & tuk & steelpan language
for sparrow & bob o rastafari chilldren & the atumpan

& those other others who have loved us lost lost sheep
when all the merchant butchers who wd slaughter .
slaughter sleep . thank you guillén césaire wilfredo

limbo. gabby. chad. odale's daughters lightning
up the sky. my mother poem mother rising from her
mountain. sir garfield sobers . caribbean stars

Bamako Poem

At Timbuctu atop the oldest mosque
an ostrich egg still marks & mocks the moon
Timbuctu is a desert of buildings

When the rain falls. there is no more desert
or rather there are no more buildings
only desert

At Bamako. the shak-shak trees
along the River Niger greet the dawn
The egg of the moon at Djenne

is the oldest mosque in the world

Coming off the long stone bridge
across this passage of the River Niger
the hulls of the boabab trees are small houses

of the poor & store places for wood. charcoal. planks
of wood. tins. cloth. beggars. old cast
-off soldiers ruined by the harmattan

ten thousand petit-malis come over this stone bridge
each morning
from far away as Koulikou by car

by bicycle. on motor scooter
- plenty car & motor scooter
- and of course most of the thousands

- mostly tall thin & unsmiling men
from distant unseen alligator villages. dark ridges
of residual forest

far out on the Saheel horizon
- walk in out of the long coarse cloth
of the encroaching desert

The Banks Hotels the Airline Offices
the Ambassie de France
& the marble Government offices like palaces

- new drops of Timbuctu
- receive them reel them reel them in
from the red dust red dust hanamanta

already rising in the heat of day

A girl. a little shave-head five year old
w/ golden earrings blinking
in short blue fading poplin dress

gathered up at the butterfly bambara shoulders
into two poppin
puffs. cute tucked-in waist & with her panties show

-ing what may be the latest gamine style
along the edges of the desert

On strong young slender dusty legs
she stops to stoop into the gutter
where the stone bridge welcome ends

near where a group of cement
-stain construction workers sit
& picks up. in like triumph

to her turning-to-her brother. a little scarcely older
the round & pale blue plastic cover
of an ice cream can

- what can you call these plastic round
containers - not 'tin' not 'can'
'container' really is too vogue. too vague

so far from Timbuctu

- but notice how she doesn't care
she knows x/actly what they'll do
she has high plans for it this dusty

morning day. as if she'd gone out shopping
early for a bargain piece
of tie-dye cloth made by the Serra women

or for a brand new shining aluminium kettle
& has found its peace

Along the sidewalk now the two
. sister & scarcely older bro
the two so close together

step in step. ticking together like bi
-cycle clicks
- only a pair of loving sibs

cd run as one like this in this hard life
of little fatten flesh over their Mali ribs
knowing the same passion mother's milk

her hip & grip of market cloth. the same small smelly narrow
pallet in the straw hut thatch
the same dog barks & rustles in the millet dark

the same long hazy silky view
of distant mountains & Limaru nearer to your heart

their four legs pedal off
her little shoulders pump
-ing young & hopeful in the light blue poplin dress

high. puffed up at the shoulders
like she high. five. in fives so far from Timbuctu
this pure Bamako katatora morning

The Nansetoura of CowPastor

From what far coast of Africa to this brown strip
of pasture on this coral limestone ridge
cast up some three miles from the burning sea

the grave
hidden within the clump of prickly man
-peaba & red cordea trees & countless clammacherry

the spider warned me of her entry
tried to prevent my photograph
ruin three lenses brek down the hi-tec pentax

cameraderie

i click the picture with a simple borrowed kodax
it burrowed through the dark & brought us this
past midnights with yr silent humming

the musky smell of turning in yr sweaty bed
the coir whispering of springs still centuries away
no water in these wells the cistern empty

the memory forlorn. its head axe off
yr sweet mouth bash & brutalize
my sister mother o my aunt my ancestor

the one eye sunk away from history . all down yr neck
along the spine now welted w/ the busha blows
yr back a modern mural of distress

the whip of auctioneers

gold bangle in yr ear. a nugget
in yr nostril. it is this other eye that blows my mind
wind in a torch you blaze upon me from yr baleful

stare. suns i have never known. world i can
never never never travel
yet you can tell me this. you tell me this

no calabash or flower on my grave no nine night wake no
forty days of journey through the salt lagoon No fru- >it
to heal this lips No okra at my hips. What happen >
>here to me is like you vomit like a rodent in Kaneshi >

market. Three hundred years I staring here under this
spider web & bush. ananse at my door of herbs. and no-
(w) you come disturb me with yr camera destroy the ru-
in of my spiral with yr flash. O watch me now. my chi-

ld my nephew flesh of my flash great great grandbroth-er
from this other world. You think they dispossessing
you? You tink you tall? you think you mouttamassiman
Rasta. reckon you rave? You say you writin poem about

slave You evva hear what Nanny tell de backra bout she
black backside? But looka yu dough nuh! Look wha be
<come a you! A buckra halfwhite backsite bwoy. eatin >
dah backra culture dah backra culture eatin you!

gyabiriw

Say wha?
De man you say is man you say doan understann?
Too many christels in yr engine?
Yu brain like windmill spinnin widdout cane

De caatwhip cut yu tong
Write this in flesh before the next red season brunn
Doan write it down in coral That is water
Write it in my body berry burnin coal

gyaNyamebiriw
gyaNyamebiriw gyaNyamebiriw

Only under God the fire
But only from my bosomtwa
- Yu tink i sick yu tink i slack - yo know whe bosomtwa? - wha
Call it so?

Only from my bosomtwa i tell you-
And the chilldren chilldren of these wounds-
The liberation

>>>

CowPastor March 2000.
*The sacred lake of the Asante is Bosomtwi. **Bosom** means sacred & secret; **twi** is the name of the*
*language of the Asante. **twa** refers to the female sexual organ. In vodoun, **bosou twa/hosou twa kòn***
is a charm, fetish, talisman, mkissi

Xângo at the Summer Solstice

for Oya

Xângo cyaan go no far-
ther. all winter long he store the sounds you hear now in
these man-
dolins. all through the cold hard dark he labour for this light

& now he find it on im lip. he blow the flute he string
im lute im rise & go again looking for his Oya
of the after. noon . im rose im pain the pale flame
of im sunset in the western tree

She sits now in the harmattan. surrendering to all this
green . heedless of headlong papers todlers lovers
she cannot ever quite ig. nore inside this Park
but even now if you look closer.   beyond the book

she's murmur-

ing. beyond the canefields of the hair she's still up-
braiding in the mirror she is canvass-
ing.   beyond the language of the summer's clock-
work warm & curl she's bearing to the water

you will already see the shadows

even by the lakeside
even by the fountain
even by the footfall

even by the cart that sells snowball ice-cream sky-juice
& coca-cola
even within the broadcast service of the plane trees
even within the holocaust of hot hibiscus bushes
even within the deepest brocade russets of the dawn

Each year upon this longest day
lover of leaf-light. golden beyond

the zodiac. emerald in pisces. indigo
in platinegro. when he feel strongest. most certain

most   lion   most
light-

ning. most royal. most arrow. most àxé. most Xângo

when she's most loyal jasmine
most crest & silver-

shed. most mellow full moon rising

there will be this cloud this sudden colour downfall
cold & pouring .   bright & fading

each year upon this longest day. these lovers mourning

"Soulless Machine." Digital illustration by Angelo Rombley © 1999.

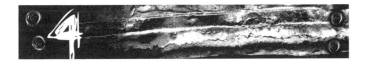

Agoue

a sequence for
VOICE, CHORAL CHORUS, MUSIC
& VODOUNISTAS

the music is Im Brooks. the vision is Temne Callender. the painting Gérard Valsin

first there is this frost and it was light
blue almost white
like cloud. icing of furushima
and then it was real cloud. like the blue

mountains

and then there are two loaves
of land. brown. w/ straight
lines in them. running up out of the dark

water

and these loaves are a distant island
like humps of a brontosaurus. w/out its head
or tail. sailing into the true

water

and the water is serene like peace and make a straight
line like anguilla
like ink under that scaly island

and there is the faintest breath of wind
upon these waters
so that it make no waves

only a gentle heave
or heaven where there would be fry
or shrimp or louvres

.

and then the fish

jump
silver. w/ red torch
light eyes . and fins shining like steel terraces

or lovers

out of the palm trees green

and then the seven
brothers of the rain-
bow. also

fish

jump straight up up up in-
to the air . that is not there

two

from the one

tree

one

from the x-
act other

and in the centre
of the purple
tuning now softly to light

in-
digo blue
dissolve of the darkness of milk

are the four

w/ leopard stops and scissor
tails all
-most in air. all

-most in water
brothers flying from branches to irie

and as they fly

. not flying . not falling .

but like flow
-ing
flow
-ing

.

here is the king . king of kings

.

iya

.

w/ the world's king. dooms re-
volving round him in cycles
and the great black golden rod
that is his staff & sceptre
emblazon in im silent head
im right hann offering to us the leaves & fishes
of his peace

and he is clothe all over like a great wide baptist
prophet rise
-ing from the flow
of water
in an obelisk of stars & ermine green
& bota beads & twinkellin sankofa
wrap around about im neck

damballa

and it is like a wind of red is sloping round im shoulder
in these royals
and like a torch of wind on water . that
sun-
light smile . o hallelujah
on im face(s)
and the great wide eye of world stare forth upon us
from him silent dread

an so he stann there still & upright . taller
than the palm
trees

in a great frieze of worshippers
in the chalk

(y)
pond

w/in the lighted water
pool

w/in the rising plate & table of what is now his heaven
land

.

and this great white spinning bowl
of daughters hounsi worshippers
on their pale howl
of island

wafer and floating bread of sound
between two threes that now are four
coiled coconuts . shakpana skein of dark

                          -ness . wind-
          drinkers . lianas of the salt & song & sea
                          & water

     dark bolom bodies stamp. ing w/ the holy mark
                  of agoue agoue agoue agoue
          daughters . dark daughters . wordless of sound

                        singing singing

              circle themselves into stillness
           their link hands raised to their chins
                      in their wonders

     vvvv in that circle . under the impact of wonder vvvv

                     their patakin feet
          black under the grain of their garments
          mov. ing inwards to ollage . great turtle

                   sea shell of passion

              raw red red mouth of erzulie
                black seeds of the melon
          four garnets of cyandle burning to whisp. ers
                        of thunder

                             .

          but no sound come from this circle of sand
                        white vision
              of dreamers . white drizzle of dancers

     altho there's a great shout of xângo echoing here
          as if a great halo has been dug into the dark
                      its head bleed-

              ing to silence & harp. less & dead

                             .

                                                    67

and there are kyeremaa drummers
under the trees
leaning back from their dreams
under their straw
hats . eyes closed to the stone

of their flesh & the fish
of the sky in the palm
trees
& the hounsi now prostrate like swimmers
through flame & the sword & the banners

yemajaa

their hands like a great wind over the brown
desert skin & the dry irie wood & blood
of their shaka & plein-
cyaas & drum-
bell

& the king watch them all from his power
out of the pools of his eye
in his silence & regency
in his dread & the red of his chains

.

& it is this the fish are flying over
whisps. cirrus cirrus cirrus. twist-
ed against the

blue

.

it is to this
the rivermaids will swim towards
across the shallow water of anegada

.

& those in blue . on that island . prostrate . floating
on sand
toes in the bright coral . pushing off . eyes close
breath held-in & hope-

full

hands stretch. ing straight starlight before them
believers far out in the night where sleep
narrows

swimming from agwe to agoue to gorée to dark

.

these then i begin to know
on this ledge
of land at the end of the proof like a prophet
of dream

listening listening listening myal

.

so it is you who see me
brother un. brother
beneath this land that is as clear as window
floating towards you out of ijs eye now closed

& water

pool
w/ its stream. ing hair & the gold fish
burning burning burning to diamint
the green unstammering glisteners

& this red boat call **echo** call **echo** call **echo**
fragile & patient here . by the green
shore of mirrors . by the

four

w/ the strapped oar lapping the cool
lapping against the waves & the ewer of silence
waiting . not waiting . here . and not

here

ready for vowels of glistance
& resting . resisting
against all these edges . as if for the long
journey . as if from the long journey
as if ravage & ready for pebble & twinkle
& music & stars

& so this small shell of sound
moored by the wrecked
oysters
by the green spikes of bushes
their mouths cracked open like frogs
dumb frozen from humus to humps

this **echo** hear i call see i face lift up from the salt
waters

agoue
agoue
agoue
agoue

catch

i hand to the rope
hanging from i hear all afternoon
the music in fragile hull of bone & new & blossom
gleam & kingdom come
& push off through splinters & sparks of yr poem
towards the distance island of sound